RUGBY UNION QUIZ BOOK

NEW, UPDATED EDITION!

THE RUGBY UNION QUIZ BOOK

NEW, UPDATED EDITION!

MATTHEW JONES

y Lolfa

First edition: 2015
Second, updated edition: 2023
© Matthew Jones & Y Lolfa Cyf., 2023

Cover design: Y Lolfa

ISBN: 978 1 80099 397 6

Published and printed in Wales
on paper from well-maintained forests by
Y Lolfa Cyf., Talybont, Ceredigion SY24 5HE
e-mail ylolfa@ylolfa.com
website www.ylolfa.com
tel 01970 832 304

Introduction

The game of rugby union has developed significantly since its origins on the playing fields of Rugby School, where in 1823 William Webb Ellis picked the ball up during a game of football and ran with it. Since then we have seen rugby clubs becoming integral parts of their communities, and a thirst for the International game sees matches broadcast across the globe.

The rugby union fan has certainly been entertained over the decades with moments of scintillating skill, flair and bravery. For those who adore nothing better than a fifty-yard run finished off by a dramatic try, images of a moment of magic from a Serge Blanco, David Campese, Bryan Habana or Gerald Davies probably resonate well in the memory. Others enjoy nothing more than a tough scrum with the pure force, technical ability and aggression of eight against eight deciding supremacy.

The game has been laden with international superstars such as Jonah Lomu, Jonny Wilkinson, Gareth Edwards, Antoine Dupont and Brian O'Driscoll. This list is far from exclusive and could easily go on for several paragraphs, if not pages.

There are certain moments in life that you'll never forget, and for a hardened fan of the oval ball, a first rugby match must sit right up there – whether at a local pitch or in one of the great sporting amphitheatres of the world, such as Eden Park, Thomond Park or Twickenham.

This book is an opportunity for you to test your knowledge of the fantastic game. The questions are a mixture: some hard, others easier. There's something in here for every type of supporter. Hope you enjoy it!

Matthew Jones
July 2023

Questions

Round 1

1. Who in 2020 became the first referee to take charge of 100 Test matches when he officiated a game between France and Italy?

   a) Nigel Owens
   b) Romain Poite
   c) Jaco Peyper

2. Ireland lost 23–16 to Wales in the 2015 Six Nations Championship. Who won his 100th Irish cap on the day?

   a) Rory Best
   b) Jamie Heaslip
   c) Paul O'Connell

3. Who made his England debut at the age of 30 against Australia in 1988?

   a) Jeff Probyn
   b) Paul Ackford
   c) Wade Dooley

4. Who, in a match against England in 2018, became the first South Africa prop to earn 100 International caps?

   a) Tendai Mtawarira
   b) Steven Kitshoff
   c) Frans Malherbe

5. Who scored a try on his **New Zealand debut at Dunedin's Carisbrook against Scotland in 1990**, then scored a try on his 50th appearance – against the same opposition, at the same stadium and nearly in the same spot – six years later?

    a) Frank Bunce

    b) Olo Brown

    c) Ian Jones

6. Who was the only Scottish International to play for the Barbarians in their famous 23–11 victory over New Zealand in 1973?

    a) Peter Brown

    b) Gordon Brown

    c) Sandy Carmichael

7. Which side won the French championship five times during the 1990s?

    a) Toulouse

    b) Brive

    c) Biarritz

8. Who, in a game against South Africa in 2021, became the first player to captain Australia on 60 occasions?

9. Who scored 228 points in 26 British and Irish Lions matches during the 1974 tour of South Africa and the 1977 tour of New Zealand?

10. In 2012, which New Zealand International became the first player to win a World Cup, a Super Rugby title and a European Cup?

Round 2

1. In which country did the **Currie Cup** become an annual competition in 1968?

   a) South Africa
   b) Italy
   c) Argentina

2. Who, against Argentina in 2016, became the first England back to receive a red card?

   a) George Ford
   b) Danny Care
   c) Elliot Daly

3. During the 1995 Rugby World Cup, who became the first All Black to score six tries in a Test match?

   a) Jeff Wilson
   b) Jonah Lomu
   c) Marc Ellis

4. On making his debut in 2008 against Italy, which versatile back became the youngest Wallaby since Brian Ford in 1957?

   a) Digby Ioane
   b) Pat McCabe
   c) James O'Connor

5. Hollywood actor Matt Damon starred in the 2009 Clint Eastwood-directed film *Invictus*. Which former Springbok did he depict in the film?

   a) Joel Stransky
   b) Francois Pienaar
   c) André Joubert

6. Scotland beat Romania 12–6 in 1981. In the game Andy Irvine scored his 209th International point, to set a new world record. Whose record did he overtake?

   a) Don Clarke
   b) Barry John
   c) Tom Kiernan

7. Who scored a brace of tries as Wales defeated France by a record score of 21–0 in Cardiff in 1950?

   a) Ken Jones
   b) Jack Matthews
   c) Gerwyn Williams

8. Who overtook Ronan O'Gara's all-time Six Nations Championship record of 557 points, in a match against England during the 2023 tournament?

9. Who was England team manager for 49 matches from January 1988 until March 1994?

10. Which country in 2013 recorded their first back-to-back Six Nations wins since 2001?

Round 3

1. **What is the colour of Italy's home shirt?**
   a) white
   b) red
   c) blue

2. **Which former Wales flanker was head coach of Russia for the 2019 Rugby World Cup?**
   a) Mark Perego
   b) Lyn Jones
   c) Richard Webster

3. **Which 33-year-old former scrum half became France coach in 1981?**
   a) Jacques Fouroux
   b) Max Barrau
   c) Gérard Sutra

4. **Reginald Birkett, Charles Wilson and John Sutcliffe have what in common?**
   a) they all won England caps in rugby union and football
   b) they all earned International caps for the British and Irish Lions before playing for England
   c) they all played for England while serving in the army

5. **In 2022, which country won a Test series in New Zealand for the first time?**

   a) Wales

   b) Japan

   c) Ireland

6. **Ponsonby Rugby Club was founded in 1874. In which New Zealand city is the club based?**

   a) Wellington

   b) Auckland

   c) Palmerston North

7. **Who did Canada defeat 18–16 in June 1994?**

   a) France

   b) England

   c) New Zealand

8. **Whose 24-try International world record stood from 1933 until eclipsed by David Campese in 1987?**

9. **New Zealand outside half Frano Botica joined which Welsh club side in 1996?**

10. **Who was the 46-times-capped France International jailed in 2018 for robbery, violence and drunk driving, having already been to jail for the murder of his wife in 2004?**

Round 4

1. **How many changes did Warren Gatland make to his starting Wales XV during the 2023 Six Nations?**

    a) 4
    b) 11
    c) 26

2. **Speaking before the first British and Irish Lions Test against South Africa in 1997, who said, "To win for the Lions in a Test match is the ultimate. The opposition don't rate you. They don't respect you. The only way to be rated is to stick one up them."?**

    a) Jim Telfer
    b) Martin Johnson
    c) Ieuan Evans

3. **Who made 45 consecutive appearances for France from 1982 to 1987?**

    a) Serge Blanco
    b) Philippe Sella
    c) Pierre Berbizier

4. **Who did Italy defeat 19–22 away from home in the 2015 Six Nations Championship?**

    a) Ireland
    b) Wales
    c) Scotland

5. **Who was the top points scorer at the 1999 Rugby World Cup?**
    a) Gonzalo Quesada
    b) Neil Jenkins
    c) Matthew Burke

6. **Which Irish province defeated Australia for a third time with a 22–19 victory in 1992?**
    a) Ulster
    b) Munster
    c) Leinster

7. **Who became the fourth Englishman to lead his country on his Test debut when he appeared against Australia in 1984?**
    a) Nigel Melville
    b) Richard Hill
    c) Jon Hall

8. **During the 1980s, which pair of brothers became the first twins to play together for New Zealand?**

9. **Heyneke Meyer was named head coach of which country in 2012?**

10. **Which two clubs suffered mid-season suspension and relegation from the English Premiership during the 2022/23 season, due to going into administration?**

Round 5

1. **Who captained Australia to their 1991 Rugby World Cup title?**

    a) Nick Farr-Jones
    b) David Campese
    c) Rod McCall

2. **How many caps in total were won by Alain Penaud (1992–2000), Peter Clohessy (1993–2002) and Paul Thorburn (1985–1991)?**

    a) 123
    b) 169
    c) 191

3. **Who scored 1,598 points in 112 New Zealand appearances from 2003 until 2015?**

    a) Stephen Donald
    b) Colin Slade
    c) Dan Carter

4. **Which club was the first to provide 100 Internationals for the Scotland national side?**

    a) Edinburgh Wanderers
    b) Hawick
    c) London Scottish

5. **'Bloodgate' was an incident on 12 April 2009 when a Harlequins player used a blood capsule to fake an injury in a game Leinster won 6–5. Who was the player who took the capsule?**

   a) Nick Evans

   b) Tom Williams

   c) Chris Robshaw

6. **Mario Ledesma resigned as which country's head coach in 2022?**

   a) Argentina

   b) Canada

   c) Portugal

7. **Which country in 2022 won their first ever victory against Australia?**

   a) Georgia

   b) Italy

   c) Romania

8. **Selkirk outside half John Rutherford made 42 Scotland International appearances. He partnered the same scrum half on 35 of these occasions. Who was the scrum half?**

9. **Who started the 1995 Rugby World Cup final at full back for South Africa with a broken hand?**

10. **England Internationals Ray Longland, Gary Pearce and David Powell played for a combined total of 55 years for the same club. Which club was this?**

Round 6

1. **Barry John, Paul McLean and Craig Chalmers played rugby at which position?**
   a) wing
   b) outside half
   c) flanker

2. **Which ground hosted the first Rugby World Cup final in 1987?**
   a) Eden Park, Auckland
   b) Lancaster Park, Christchurch
   c) Athletic Park, Wellington

3. **In which year did London Scottish's Lindsay Renwick, Neath's Phil Pugh and Harlequins' Andy Mullins all win their only International cap?**
   a) 1985
   b) 1987
   c) 1989

4. **Richie McCaw made 148 New Zealand appearances. How many times did he captain his country?**
   a) 111
   b) 131
   c) 148

5. **Who made the most appearances (23 games) on the 1966 British and Irish Lions tour of Australia and New Zealand?**

    a) Alun Pask
    b) Delme Thomas
    c) Dewi Bebb

6. **France defeated Scotland 15–8 in the 2015 Six Nations. Who scored all of France's points, in his first tournament start?**

    a) Rory Kockott
    b) Rémi Talès
    c) Camille Lopez

7. **England defeated Wales 7–3 at Twickenham in 1923. Who set a record for England's fastest try, touching down ten seconds into the match?**

    a) Geoffrey Conway
    b) Leo Price
    c) Cyril Lowe

8. **Who kicked all of Argentina's 21 points in their 1985 draw against New Zealand?**

9. **Which Irishman was named International Rugby Board player of the year in 2001?**

10. **Who in 2018 became South Africa's first black captain?**

Round 7

1. **Which country hosted the 2019 Rugby World Cup?**

   a) Paraguay

   b) Kenya

   c) Japan

2. **In 2018, Sekope Kepu became the first prop from which country to make 100 International appearances?**

   a) Australia

   b) Wales

   c) Scotland

3. **Which country's team arrived in the United Kingdom for their 1939 tour only to find out that the Second World War had broken out, and had to return without putting on their boots?**

   a) New Zealand

   b) Australia

   c) South Africa

4. **Who scored 22 tries in 23 matches during the British and Irish Lions' 1959 tour of Australia and New Zealand?**

   a) Terry Davies

   b) Peter Jackson

   c) Tony O'Reilly

5. **Of the following, which player scored the most International points?**

    a) Michael Kiernan
    b) Bob Hiller
    c) Gavin Henson

6. **South Africa defeated Western Samoa 42–14 in 1995. Who scored four tries in the game?**

    a) Gavin Johnson
    b) Chester Williams
    c) Hendrik le Roux

7. **In 1989, who did Japan defeat 28–24 in Tokyo?**

    a) Australia
    b) Scotland
    c) Wales

8. **Which future Scarlets centre became the first player in rugby union's professional era to make his New Zealand debut before playing a game of Super Rugby?**

9. **Bath beat Leicester 16–15 in the 1996 Pilkington Cup final. Who received a six-month ban for pushing over referee Steve Lander at the end of the game?**

10. **Who was named International Rugby Board coach of the year for a record fifth time in 2011?**

Round 8

1. **Imanol Harinordoquy, Mervyn Davies and Andy Ripley were all known for playing at which position?**

    a) centre

    b) No. 8

    c) hooker

2. **Who captained Australia 55 times in 86 capped appearances from 1991 until 2001?**

    a) Jason Little

    b) Tim Horan

    c) John Eales

3. **Who co-presented the 1997 and 1998 UK series of *Gladiators* with Ulrika Jonsson?**

    a) Jeremy Guscott

    b) Ieuan Evans

    c) Scott Hastings

4. **Cardigan Fields, Headingley and Meanwood Road are grounds that have hosted England Internationals. In which city were these located?**

    a) Manchester

    b) Leeds

    c) Bristol

5. **Which Going brother scored 714 points in 130 matches for North Auckland from 1963 until 1975?**

   a) Sid
   b) Ken
   c) Brian

6. **Ireland dual International (rugby union and football) Kevin O'Flanagan played football for which of the following clubs?**

   a) Manchester United
   b) Liverpool
   c) Arsenal

7. **Peter Williams was an England rugby union International and Wales rugby league International. His father was a former Llanelli forward. What was his name?**

   a) Ossie Williams
   b) Rhys (R H) Williams
   c) Roy Williams

8. **Who was dropped from the Scotland squad prior to the 2020 Six Nations tournament as he'd missed training following an alleged drinking session?**

9. **Who in 2011 became the first New Zealand International to achieve 100 caps?**

10. **Who scored 67 tries in 124 South Africa appearances from 2004 to 2016?**

Round 9

1. **Which country wears a white home jersey?**

   a) England
   b) Ireland
   c) Wales

2. **Vern Cotter became Scotland head coach in 2014. Who held the position on an interim basis prior to this?**

   a) Gareth Jenkins
   b) Scott Johnson
   c) Mike Ruddock

3. **Who did Italy beat 23–18 at the Stadio Olimpico in the 2013 Six Nations Championship?**

   a) Ireland
   b) Wales
   c) France

4. **Wales beat Scotland 23–26 at Murrayfield in 2015. Who scored the two Welsh tries?**

   a) Leigh Halfpenny and Alex Cuthbert
   b) Rhys Webb and Jonathan Davies
   c) Gethin Jenkins and Liam Williams

5. **Who captained South Africa for the only time in his 25th and final Test, a 9–18 loss to England at Ellis Park in 1972?**

   a) Piet Greyling
   b) Syd Nomis
   c) Jan Ellis

6. **France lost 13–18 to Argentina at Stade de France in 2014. Who scored 15 points for the visitors?**

    a) Juan Martín Hernández

    b) Santiago Gonzáles Iglesias

    c) Nicolás Sánchez

7. **Who won the inaugural Women's Rugby World Cup in 1991?**

    a) USA

    b) France

    c) Netherlands

8. **Who was given a one-year matchday ban following the release of a video where he criticised the refereeing of the first Test between South Africa and the British and Irish Lions in 2021?**

9. **Who scored 645 points in 46 New Zealand Tests from 1985 until 1993?**

10. **England defeated Wales 23–19 in the 2022 Six Nations tournament. Who were the Northampton Saints clubmates that captained the two sides?**

Round 10

1. **'Rugby football is a game for gentlemen in all classes, but for no bad sportsman in any class.' This is the motto of which club?**
   - a) Hawick
   - b) Barbarians
   - c) Penarth

2. **Which of the following clubs did Rob Andrew <u>not</u> play for?**
   - a) Wasps
   - b) Nottingham
   - c) Richmond

3. **BBC commentator Bill McLaren was asked in 2002 to select his greatest-ever World XV. Who did he select at full back?**
   - a) Andy Irvine
   - b) J P R Williams
   - c) Serge Blanco

4. **Who played his last International match in 1983, having scored a record for a prop of 8 tries in 55 games?**
   - a) Graham Price
   - b) Robert Paparemborde
   - c) Mike Burton

5. **Which club set a world record by scoring 1,917 points in a 50-game season in 1988/89?**

    a) Neath

    b) Bath

    c) Dolphin

6. **Who kicked a last-minute drop goal to give Scotland a one-point victory over Italy in 2014?**

    a) Ruaridh Jackson

    b) Stuart Hogg

    c) Duncan Weir

7. **Of the following, who made the most International appearances for the British and Irish Lions?**

    a) Phil Bennett

    b) Paul O'Connell

    c) John Jeffrey

8. **Brian O'Brien had the distinction of becoming Shannon's first Ireland International in 1968. Which position did he play?**

9. **Who was named World Rugby Coach of the Year in 2012, 2013, 2014 and 2016?**

10. **Who captained victors Fiji at the 1997 and 2005 Rugby World Cup Sevens?**

Round 11

1. **Who are the 'Sea Eagles'?**

    a) Tonga

    b) Papua New Guinea

    c) France

2. **In 2013, who became the first player to exceed 1,500 points in Super Rugby?**

    a) Dan Carter

    b) Morné Steyn

    c) Tony Brown

3. **Who replaced Jason Leonard during England's 54–21 victory over Italy in 1996, becoming his country's first tactical substitute?**

    a) Graham Rowntree

    b) Rob Hardwick

    c) John Mallett

4. **Which of the following made his 100th Italy appearance in 2018?**

    a) Tommaso Benvenuti

    b) Lorenzo Cittadini

    c) Alessandro Zanni

5. **Which of the following was given the nickname 'Pinball' due to his ability to bounce off tackles?**

    a) Simon Webster

    b) Gary Armstrong

    c) Hamish Watson

6. **Who made a then world record 64th Test appearance in Wales' 20–16 victory over Ireland in 1978?**

    a) Gareth Edwards
    b) Mike Gibson
    c) Gerald Davies

7. **Which Nadi-born player ended his Fiji career in 2010 with 16 tries from 47 Internationals?**

    a) Norman Ligairi
    b) Albert Vulivuli
    c) Gaby Lovobalavu

8. **What did Rob Simmons achieve in 2019 that Stephen Larkham did in 2007 and David Campese did in 1996?**

9. **40-times-capped Scotland International Hugh McLeod was known as a one-club man. Who did he both play for and become president of?**

10. **Ireland won the 2014 Six Nations Championship. Who won the Triple Crown?**

Round 12

1. Which colour shirt did France wear in the 2015 Six Nations, for the first time since 1959?

   a) black

   b) white

   c) red

2. Lord Kew, Basil Brush and Le Hippy were nicknames given to which Welsh back-row forward?

   a) John Taylor

   b) Dai Morris

   c) Paul Ringer

3. South Africa beat Italy 101–0 in 1999. Who in the match became the first Springbok to score five tries in an International?

   a) Breyton Paulse

   b) Stefan Terblanche

   c) Robbie Fleck

4. Scotland's 35–7 victory over Wales in 2023 broke their previous 25-point winning margin record against the Welsh. Since when had this record stood?

   a) 1911

   b) 1924

   c) 1933

5. **Which member of New Zealand's 1987 Rugby World Cup-winning team had a father, Brian, who won three Test caps in the 1950s?**

    a) Sean Fitzpatrick

    b) John Gallagher

    c) Warwick Taylor

6. **In which year did Scotland gain their first Home Nations Triple Crown?**

    a) 1891

    b) 1911

    c) 1931

7. **Ireland fielded a three-quarter line of Jack Arigho, Eugene Davy, Morgan Crowe and Ned Lightfoot during their 1931 season. Which club did they all play for?**

    a) Cork Constitution

    b) Old Belvedere

    c) Lansdowne

8. **Who was the 73-times-capped Australia International who had his Wallabies contract torn up in 2019 due to comments he made about homosexuals and other groups?**

9. **At the age of 36, who became England's oldest centre when he played against his country of birth, South Africa, in 2007?**

10. **Name the Ebbw Vale back-row forward who made his Wales debut in 1977 against Ireland.**

Round 13

1. **Arorangi Cowboys and Titikaveka Bulls are clubs from which country?**

    a) Cook Islands

    b) Spain

    c) Tonga

2. **With a score of 23–8, who did Japan defeat for the first time in their history in 2013?**

    a) South Africa

    b) Wales

    c) France

3. **Who was captain of South Africa's 'Invincibles' tour of Australia in 1971, during which they never lost a game?**

    a) Piet Greyling

    b) Frik du Preez

    c) Hannes Marais

4. **Wales defeated France for a fourth consecutive time in 2015. In which year had they previously achieved this?**

    a) 1927

    b) 1957

    c) 1977

5. **Who reached the final three on the BBC's 2018 series of *Celebrity Masterchef*?**

    a) Martin Bayfield

    b) Roy Laidlaw

    c) Bobby Windsor

6. Which country was thrown out of the Five Nations for signing a television deal with Sky Sports in 1996, before being reinstated ahead of the 1997 tournament and therefore not missing a game?

    a) Wales
    b) Scotland
    c) England

7. In 2018, who became the first two Ireland players to win multiple Six Nations Grand Slams?

    a) Jack McGrath and Devin Toner
    b) Rory Best and Rob Kearney
    c) Dan Leavy and Keith Earls

8. Who made his 150th appearance for Wales in a one-point loss to Italy during the 2022 Six Nations tournament?

9. Munster defeated Australia 11–8 at Musgrave Park in 1967. Who captained Munster?

10. Which former All Black became the host of the *Brunch* programme on New Zealand's Choice TV in 2012?

Round 14

1. **In 2012, which country joined the Tri-Nations to form The Rugby Championship?**

    a) Kenya

    b) Argentina

    c) Samoa

2. **France defeated Australia 30–24 in their 1987 Rugby World Cup semi-final. Who scored the winning try?**

    a) Patrice Lagisquet

    b) Pascal Ondarts

    c) Serge Blanco

3. **In which country were New Zealand Internationals Greg Rawlinson and Andrew Mehrtens born?**

    a) India

    b) South Africa

    c) Saudi Arabia

4. **22-year-old George North in 2015 became the youngest player to earn 50 International caps. Whose record did he supersede?**

    a) Ma'a Nonu

    b) Jonny Wilkinson

    c) Joe Roff

5. **Who coached the Crusaders to five Super Rugby Championship titles from 2000 to 2008?**

    a) Robbie Deans

    b) Wayne Smith

    c) Peter Sloane

6. **The British and Irish Lions opened their 2021 tour with a first ever match against which country?**

    a) Japan
    b) Portugal
    c) Chile

7. **In 1981, who became the first northern-hemisphere side and also the last non-international side to win the Hong Kong Sevens?**

    a) Public School Wanderers
    b) Barbarians
    c) Co-optimists

8. **Lawrence Dallaglio won 85 caps in his England career. Which other two countries did he qualify to represent?**

9. **Wales selected a pair of uncapped outside halves for their 1978 tour of Australia. Who were they?**

10. **Scotland flanker Rob Wainwright was a double Cambridge blue. One was for rugby union. What was the other for?**

Round 15

1. **Which country did Nick Popplewell, Jim Staples and Niall Hogan represent?**

    a) Samoa

    b) USA

    c) Ireland

2. **Stuart Lancaster was named permanent England head coach in 2012. Which country did he represent in his playing career at under-19 and under-20 levels?**

    a) Scotland

    b) Wales

    c) Kenya

3. **Who was South Africa's first captain following their readmission to International rugby in 1992?**

    a) Heinrich Rodgers

    b) Uli Schmidt

    c) Naas Botha

4. **Which country defeated France 12–17 in the group stages of the 2007 Rugby World Cup?**

    a) Argentina

    b) Wales

    c) Fiji

5. **Who scored his first International try on his 50th appearance for France in a match against Wales in 2023?**

    a) Julien Marchand

    b) Uini Antonio

    c) Cyril Baille

6. **Who captained Australia to their first Bledisloe Cup victory on New Zealand soil in 1949?**

    a) Rex Mossop

    b) Jack Blomley

    c) Trevor Allan

7. **Who was the top try scorer at the 2019 Rugby World Cup?**

    a) Josh Adams

    b) Makazole Mapimpi

    c) Kotaro Matsushima

8. **Pedro Carvalho became his country's first ever try scorer in a Rugby World Cup during a 56–10 loss to Scotland in 2007. Which country did he play for?**

9. **Who made his New Zealand debut in 1974 at the age of 29, captaining his country in all of the ten Tests that he played?**

10. **Who made his England debut in 2017, 33 years after his father's only England cap?**

Round 16

1. **Which country won a third Rugby World Cup in 2019?**

   a) South Africa

   b) Wales

   c) Japan

2. **In 2023 Scotland won a third consecutive Calcutta Cup. When was the last time they achieved this?**

   a) 1992

   b) 1982

   c) 1972

3. **Who set a national record by captaining France on 34 occasions between 1977 and 1984?**

   a) Gérard Cholley

   b) Jean-Pierre Rives

   c) Jean-Claude Skrela

4. **England defeated the Netherlands 110–0 in November 1998. Who set a national record of 15 conversions on the day?**

   a) Paul Grayson

   b) Jonny Wilkinson

   c) Tim Stimpson

5. **Which Welsh front-row forward scored nine tries in 41 British and Irish Lions matches from 1955 to 1962?**

   a) Billy Williams

   b) Bryn Meredith

   c) Courtney Meredith

6. **Which side became the first opponents of the Barbarians, on 27 December 1890?**

   a) Cardiff

   b) Devon County

   c) Hartlepool Rovers

7. **Which scrum half played in 12 Tests for Australia from 1958 to 1959, then went on to earn the same number of caps for New Zealand from 1961 to 1964?**

   a) Ken McMullen

   b) Brian Cox

   c) Des Connor

8. **Who missed a straightforward penalty kick in front of the posts for Scotland as they lost 6–9 to England in their 1991 Rugby World Cup semi-final?**

9. **'Viet Gwent' was the nickname given to which Welsh club's front row during the 1970s?**

10. **Who scored 20 points on his New Zealand debut, against Wales at Hamilton in 2003?**

Round 17

1. **Girvan Dempsey scored 19 tries in 82 International appearances. Which country did he represent?**

    a) Samoa

    b) Ireland

    c) Scotland

2. **Who, in 2020, captained Argentina to a first ever victory over New Zealand?**

    a) Pablo Matera

    b) Nicolás Sánchez

    c) Julián Montoya

3. **Newlands is a stadium that hosted its first South Africa International match in 1891. In which city is it located?**

    a) Polokwane

    b) Nelspruit

    c) Cape Town

4. **Which member of New Zealand's 2007 Rugby World Cup squad had a father called Frank who earned 17 Test caps for the All Blacks from 1976 to 1981?**

    a) Leon MacDonald

    b) Byron Kelleher

    c) Anton Oliver

5. **Prop Ron Jacobs made a record 470 club appearances from 1949 to 1966. Which club did he represent during this period?**

    a) Northampton

    b) Moseley

    c) Coventry

6. **Oscar-winning actor Javier Bardem won under-16 and under-18 caps for which country?**

    a) Spain

    b) Argentina

    c) Uruguay

7. **Who scored 8 tries in 12 matches on the 1974 British and Irish Lions tour of South Africa?**

    a) Gordon Brown

    b) Willie John McBride

    c) Chris Ralston

8. **Who earned his 100th Scotland cap during the 2023 Six Nations tournament?**

9. **In football, Niko Kirwan scored his first goal for New Zealand in a match against Bahrain in 2021. Who is his rugby union International father?**

10. **Arturo Bergamasco won four caps for Italy in the 1970s. Who are his two International sons?**

Round 18

1. **Wycliff Palu, Scott Quinnell and Anthony Foley have all made over 50 appearances for their country. Which position would you associate with them?**
    a) hooker
    b) scrum half
    c) No. 8

2. **Which former International held the role of Argentina's Minister of Sport from 1996 until 1999?**
    a) Gustavo Milano
    b) Hugo Porta
    c) Raul Loyola

3. **What did the following hookers have in common: Bath's Andy Long, Newbridge's Ken Waters and Hawick's Jim Hay?**
    a) They were one-cap Internationals.
    b) They won a British and Irish Lions cap before playing for their country.
    c) They won International caps at two different positions, but not as a hooker.

4. **Which Australian was named the inaugural International Rugby Board Coach of the Year in 2001?**
    a) Greg Smith
    b) Eddie Jones
    c) Rod Macqueen

5. **Which Whitelock brother became New Zealand's eighth International centurion in 2018?**

   a) Sam

   b) George

   c) Luke

6. **Australia International Israel Folau made his debut for which country in 2022?**

   a) Singapore

   b) Tonga

   c) Cook Islands

7. **Walter Rees became Secretary of the Welsh Rugby Union in 1896. How long did he stay in this position?**

   a) 32 years

   b) 42 years

   c) 52 years

8. **Who retired in 1973 as Ireland's most-capped player (55 games), having also made the most appearances as captain (22 games)?**

9. **Who scored 12 tries in 33 Scotland matches from 1955 until 1962?**

10. **Gysie Pienaar earned 13 caps for South Africa in the early 1980s. His son made his International debut in August 2006. Who is the younger Pienaar?**

Round 19

1. **Who scored 1,083 points in 128 Ireland appearances?**

   a) David Humphreys

   b) Paddy Wallace

   c) Ronan O'Gara

2. **Forward Jamie Joseph played International rugby for which two countries?**

   a) Scotland and Samoa

   b) New Zealand and Japan

   c) Wales and Papua New Guinea

3. **Wales romped to a 51–3 victory over Scotland in 2014. Which member of the Scotland side was sent off 23 minutes into the game for a late shoulder charge on Dan Biggar?**

   a) Stuart Hogg

   b) Dougie Fife

   c) Alex Dunbar

4. **In 2022, which side became the first from South Africa to win the United Rugby Championship?**

   a) Lions

   b) Bulls

   c) Stormers

5. **Who retired in 1967 at the age of 38 as Australia's most-capped player with 41 appearances?**

   a) Jim Lenehan

   b) Tony Miller

   c) Eddie Stapleton

6. **Full back Ken Scotland made 27 International appearances for the Scotland rugby union team. Which other sport did he play internationally?**

   a) cricket
   b) rugby league
   c) basketball

7. **Coventry wing Timothy Dalton won his only England cap in 1969 during an 8–3 victory over Scotland. He became the first Englishman to earn a cap as a substitute. Who did he replace in the game?**

   a) Keith Fielding
   b) Rodney Webb
   c) Bob Hiller

8. **The British and Irish Lions drew the first Test of their 1971 tour against New Zealand 14–14. Which Welshman kicked a fantastic 45-metre drop goal, the only one of his illustrious career, during the game?**

9. **George Lindsay set a Home Nations record by scoring five tries in a single match when he appeared against Wales in 1887. Which country did he play for?**

10. **Who presented the Webb Ellis Cup to Francois Pienaar at the end of the 1995 Rugby World Cup final?**

Round 20

1. **Who made his 100th and final appearance for Wales against the Barbarians in 2012?**
   - a) Martyn Williams
   - b) Lee Byrne
   - c) Dwayne Peel

2. **Joe Schmidt became head coach for which country in 2013?**
   - a) Samoa
   - b) Ireland
   - c) Namibia

3. **Who lost 38–23 to England in the 1994 Women's Rugby World Cup final?**
   - a) Canada
   - b) Wales
   - c) USA

4. **Which Australia back-row forward played in 59 Tests, including 4 as captain, from 1980 until 1991?**
   - a) David Codey
   - b) Simon Poidevin
   - c) Troy Coker

5. **Mark Keyworth, Tony Swift and Maurice Colclough won England caps while playing for which Welsh side?**
   - a) Aberavon
   - b) Ebbw Vale
   - c) Swansea

6. **Who were the inaugural winners of the Hong Kong Sevens Cup in 1976?**

    a) Fiji
    b) Cantabrians
    c) Indonesia

7. **Which Ireland forward, who made his International debut against USA in 2017, is the great-grandson of an Irish politician and Easter Rising revolutionary of the same name?**

    a) Jacob Stockdale
    b) Andrew Porter
    c) James Ryan

8. **Which winger of Polynesian descent scored 71 points in 38 All Black Tests from 1970 until 1978?**

9. **Who was Wales' soon-to-be sacked head coach when they suffered a humiliating 13–12 loss at home to Georgia in 2022?**

10. **Who set a Canada record of 491 points in a 55-match International career from 1986 until 1999?**

Round 21

1. **What is the colour of Tonga's home shirt?**

    a) red

    b) blue

    c) white

2. **The Highlanders play home matches in which of the following cities?**

    a) Auckland

    b) Dunedin

    c) Napier

3. **Which club side won the French championship six times during the 1970s?**

    a) Béziers

    b) Narbonne

    c) Dax

4. **Who captained Japan to a 28–21 victory over Scotland in the 2019 Rugby World Cup?**

    a) Michael Leitch

    b) Luke Thompson

    c) Shota Horie

5. **What on-field controversy occurred during England's 35–22 victory over Samoa in the 2003 Rugby World Cup?**

    a) Hooker Mark Regan played for England. Due to a red card in the previous match he was suspended, but the England management didn't realise and selected him for the match.

b) England played 30 seconds with 16 players on the field.

c) Flanker Neil Back illegally used his hands in an attacking scrum, resulting in England incorrectly being awarded a penalty try.

6. **Sean Fitzpatrick suffered an ear bite when playing against South Africa in 1994. The aggressor received an 18-month ban. Who was he?**

   a) Tiaan Strauss

   b) Krynauw Otto

   c) Johan le Roux

7. **Who appeared in ITV's 2019 series of *I'm a Celebrity... Get Me Out of Here!*?**

   a) James Haskell

   b) Gareth Edwards

   c) Gavin Hastings

8. **Who in 2022 became the third Irishman to be awarded the World Rugby Player of the Year award?**

9. **Which member of Wales' 1965 Triple Crown-winning side signed for the Buffalo Bills American football side as a specialist kicker in 1971?**

10. **Jim Thompson scored a try on his Scotland A debut in 2008. Who was his Scottish rugby hall of fame grandfather?**

Round 22

1. **Captain David Irwin led which side to a 15–13 victory over Australia in 1984?**

    a) Ebbw Vale

    b) Ulster

    c) South of Scotland

2. **Which country defeated New Zealand 43–31 in a 1999 Rugby World Cup semi-final?**

    a) France

    b) Wales

    c) South Africa

3. **The Cavaliers were an unofficial New Zealand team that toured South Africa in 1986. Who was the team's coach?**

    a) Colin Meads

    b) Ian Kirkpatrick

    c) Sid Going

4. **In a match against Scotland in 2023, who became the first player to receive a second Six Nations Championship red card?**

    a) Tadhg Furlong

    b) Dan Cole

    c) Mohamed Haouas

5. **England defeated Wales 11–6 at Twickenham in 1910. Who set a national record for fastest-scoring debut try scorer by crossing the whitewash 75 seconds into the match?**

    a) Bert Solomon
    b) Fred Chapman
    c) Edgar Mobbs

6. **Who scored Australia's only try in their 1991 Rugby World Cup final victory over England?**

    a) Marty Roebuck
    b) Tony Daly
    c) Willie Ofahengaue

7. **BBC Wales awarded their first Wales Sports Personality of the Year award in 1954. Who won it?**

    a) Roy John
    b) Cliff Morgan
    c) Ken Jones

8. **The English County Championship competition was renamed in 2007 to honour a former International. Who was it named after?**

9. **What links England's Roger Creed, Scotland's Jim Hamilton and Ireland's Luke Fitzgerald?**

10. **New Zealand defeated Samoa 71–13 in 1999. Which pair of brothers found themselves on opposing sides that day?**

Round 23

1. **Huw Jones made his International debut in 2016. Which country did he play for?**
   a) South Africa
   b) Scotland
   c) Wales

2. **Simon Raiwalui, Emori Katalau and Kele Leawere are all Fiji Internationals. Which position would you associate with them?**
   a) scrum half
   b) full back
   c) second row

3. **Who led Ireland to their first Grand Slam in 1948?**
   a) Karl Mullen
   b) Barney Mullan
   c) Jack Kyle

4. **Mike Campbell-Lamerton relinquished the British and Irish Lions captaincy for two Tests on their 1966 tour because he felt he wasn't playing well enough. Who was given the captaincy for those matches?**
   a) Dewi Bebb
   b) Delme Thomas
   c) David Watkins

5. **England Internationals William Milton, Reggie Schwartz and Reginald Hands share what in common?**

    a) They won their first cap while still at school.

    b) They were also cricket Internationals for South Africa.

    c) They each earned caps for England while representing five different clubs.

6. **Which Australian gained 9 caps in a 13-week International career, which culminated in winning the 1991 Rugby World Cup final?**

    a) Bob Egerton

    b) Paul Carozza

    c) Darren Junee

7. **Which country, led by captain Agustín Creevy, defeated South Africa in 2018?**

    a) Namibia

    b) Uruguay

    c) Argentina

8. **Brothers Dolf, Jaap and Martiens Bekker were all International rugby players. Which country did they represent?**

9. **Romain Ntamack made his France debut in 2019 against Wales. Who is his 46-times-capped father?**

10. **Wales beat England 21–19 in Cardiff in 1981. Who scored all 19 points for the visitors?**

Round 24

1. **In 1970, who became the first All Black to play in 50 Tests?**

   a) Ian Clarke

   b) Colin Meads

   c) Kelvin Tremain

2. **Craig Chalmers, Keith Robertson and Jim Telfer all played for which club side?**

   a) Stirling County

   b) Melrose

   c) Boroughmuir

3. **In a European Challenge Cup match against Dragons in 2023, Johnny Matthews became the first player from which side to score five tries in a game?**

   a) Gloucester

   b) Ospreys

   c) Glasgow Warriors

4. **Which of the following Wales players made the most Test appearances for the British and Irish Lions?**

   a) John Taylor

   b) Jeff Squire

   c) Derek Quinnell

5. **Which future Wallaby became Australia's youngest ever rugby league International when he played for the Kangaroos against New Zealand in 2007?**

   a) Israel Folau

   b) Joe Tomane

   c) Henry Speight

6. **Which club won the French championship in 2009 for the first time in 54 years?**

   a) Grenoble

   b) Colomiers

   c) Perpignan

7. **Wales defeated France 13–20 at Stade de France in 2015. Who scored his first International try on his 31st appearance in a Wales shirt in the match?**

   a) Dan Biggar

   b) Luke Charteris

   c) Taulupe Faletau

8. **In which Irish city would you find Thomond Park?**

9. **Who set a South Africa record of 127 International caps when he made his final appearance against Argentina in 2015?**

10. **Jeff Wilson scored 234 points in 60 New Zealand Test matches. In which other sport did he represent his country?**

Round 25

1. **Which of the following players has the same name as an American boxer who held the title of World Heavyweight Champion from 1919 until 1926?**
    a) Mervyn Davies
    b) Jack Dempsey
    c) Will Carling

2. **Which Wales forward earned 46 caps in an International career from 1985 until 1995?**
    a) Mike Griffiths
    b) David Bryant
    c) Phil Davies

3. **Which of the following South Africa scrum halves earned the highest number of caps?**
    a) Piet Uys
    b) Dawie de Villiers
    c) Dick Lockyear

4. **On 18 April 1892 Stade Français hosted the first game on continental Europe for an English team. Which of the following was the pioneering side that won the game by four converted tries to nil?**
    a) Rosslyn Park
    b) Oxford University
    c) Blackheath

5. **Will Genia made his 110th and final Australia appearance in 2019. How many International tries has he scored?**

    a) 1
    b) 10
    c) 20

6. **In which country was the Escott Shield first competed for in 1913 and won by the Pacific club?**

    a) Fiji
    b) Japan
    c) Tonga

7. **Which International hooker was jailed for six months in 1995 for fracturing an opponent's jaw?**

    a) Louis Armary
    b) Nigel Meek
    c) Tom Lawton

8. **Diego Magno in 2022 became which country's first Test centurion?**

9. **In 2011, who became the second Argentine to be inducted into the International Rugby Board hall of fame?**

10. **Ray Dalton and his son Andy were both New Zealand Internationals. Which of them won the most caps?**

Round 26

1. **Which country performs the Haka war dance before International matches?**

    a) Australia

    b) New Zealand

    c) Japan

2. **Keven Mealamu, Stephen Moore and Ross Ford have all made more than 100 International appearances. Which position did they play?**

    a) flanker

    b) full back

    c) hooker

3. **In 1999, who became the first Scotland player to score a try in all four Five Nations games in a season?**

    a) Gregor Townsend

    b) John Leslie

    c) Kenny Logan

4. **How many caps in total were won by Malcolm O'Kelly (1997–2009), Mark Taylor (1994–2005) and Olivier Roumat (1989–1996)?**

    a) 205

    b) 238

    c) 263

5. **Which former International captain was elected to represent the Australian Capital Territory in the Australian Senate in 2022?**

   a) Mark Ella
   b) Nick Farr-Jones
   c) David Pocock

6. **Who was the only member of England's squad to play every minute of their 2003 Rugby World Cup-winning campaign?**

   a) Ben Kay
   b) Lawrence Dallaglio
   c) Trevor Woodman

7. **One-cap Wales Internationals Gordon Britton, Laurie Daniel and Roy Burnett all played for which club side?**

   a) Ebbw Vale
   b) Pontypool
   c) Newport

8. **South Africa International scrum half Faf de Klerk made 100 appearances for which English side from 2017 to 2022?**

9. **Following Gareth Edwards' famous try for the Barbarians against the All Blacks in 1973, who in the BBC commentary said, "If the greatest writer of the written word would have written that story, no one would have believed it."?**

10. **Which French side appointed Ronan O'Gara as their head coach in 2019?**

Round 27

1. **Ellis Park is a stadium located in which city?**

    a) Johannesburg
    b) Port Elizabeth
    c) Kimberley

2. **Luke McLean made his International debut in June 2008. Which country did he represent when taking to the field that day?**

    a) Italy
    b) Samoa
    c) Tonga

3. **Who earned 92 Wales caps in an International career from 1989 until 2004?**

    a) Scott Gibbs
    b) John Davies
    c) Gareth Llewellyn

4. **Which of the following countries did <u>not</u> appear at the 2010 Women's Rugby World Cup?**

    a) Sweden
    b) Fiji
    c) Kazakhstan

5. **Former Pontypridd coach Lynn Howells became director of rugby for which national team in 2012?**

    a) Romania
    b) Portugal
    c) Japan

6. **Alexander Obolensky became the first England player to score a brace of tries against the All Blacks on his debut in 1936. Robert Lloyd became the second to do this in 1967. Who became the third in 2008?**

    a) Dan Hipkiss

    b) Topsy Ojo

    c) Ugo Monye

7. **In 1857, which was the first club to be founded in Scotland?**

    a) Glasgow Academicals

    b) West of Scotland

    c) Edinburgh Academicals

8. **Who defeated Clarence Tillman in 2012 to become New Zealand's heavyweight boxing champion?**

9. **Following a high-profile switch from rugby league, who made five appearances for England in a rugby union career which spanned one year, from 2014 until 2015?**

10. **Australia's 2015 Rugby World Cup squad contained two players who didn't ply their trade on home soil. Both played for Toulon in France. Matt Giteau was one of them. Who was the other?**

Round 28

1. **Which country won the first four Commonwealth Games Sevens tournaments from 1998 to 2010?**

    a) Fiji

    b) New Zealand

    c) Scotland

2. **South Africa prop Tendai Mtawarira made his debut against Wales in 2008. By which nickname is he better known?**

    a) T-bone

    b) Gonzo

    c) Beast

3. **David Denton, Bobby Skinstad and Takudzwa Ngwenya were all born in which country?**

    a) Zimbabwe

    b) Burkina Faso

    c) Kenya

4. **Hoylake Rugby Club boasts which James Bond actor as a former player?**

    a) Roger Moore

    b) Timothy Dalton

    c) Daniel Craig

5. **When Italy took on Portugal in 2022, who became the first female referee to officiate a match featuring a Tier One men's side?**

   a) Hollie Davidson

   b) Sara Cox

   c) Joy Neville

6. **Which 30-times-capped Australian forward was awarded the Order of the British Empire in 1971, became Lord Mayor of Sydney in 1973, was knighted in 1976 and made a Companion of the Order of Australia in 1990?**

   a) Jim Walsh

   b) Nicholas Shehadie

   c) Peter Fenwicke

7. **Andy Nicol, Richie Vernon and Jamie Ritchie were all born in which city?**

   a) Cork

   b) London

   c) Dundee

8. **Stade Marcel-Michelin is the home ground for which club side?**

9. **In 2017, which Sale Sharks flanker became the youngest forward to represent England since 1912?**

10. **Which country required a last-minute penalty to scrape a 3–3 draw against Munster at Musgrave Park in 1973?**

Round 29

1. **England Internationals Henry Paul, Lesley Vainikolo and Shontayne Hape were all rugby league Internationals prior to their move to union. Which country did they represent in the 13-man code?**
    a) Samoa
    b) New Zealand
    c) Scotland

2. **The book *Talk of the Toony* was released in 2007. Whose autobiography was it?**
    a) Kenny Logan
    b) Jim Telfer
    c) Gregor Townsend

3. **Which of the following finished his New Zealand career with a national record of 49 tries, achieved in 61 Test appearances?**
    a) Doug Howlett
    b) Christian Cullen
    c) Joe Rokocoko

4. **What do South Africa Internationals Basie Vivier, Wynand Claassen and Corné Krige have in common?**
    a) They were born in Scotland.
    b) They captained the Springboks on their debut.
    c) They have each represented South Africa while playing for four different sides.

5. **Which of the following scored the most Test tries for the British and Irish Lions?**

    a) Seán O'Brien

    b) Rory Underwood

    c) Gerald Davies

6. **Roland Bertranne set a French record in the 1970s by playing in the most consecutive Tests. How many matches did he play during this run?**

    a) 36

    b) 41

    c) 46

7. **Who in 1980 became the first Shannon player to represent the British and Irish Lions?**

    a) Colm Tucker

    b) Brendan Foley

    c) Gerry McLoughlin

8. **How many Scotland defenders did Ieuan Evans overcome to score a famous try in Wales' 25–20 win in 1988?**

9. **Which Irish province did John Muldoon represent a record 327 times from 2003 until 2018?**

10. *Wild Women Of Wongo* **was a 1950s Hollywood film. Which former Wales International played the role of the King of Wongo?**

Round 30

1. **Denis Dallan, Alessandro Troncon and Cristian Stoica have all played International rugby for which country?**
   a) Ireland
   b) Italy
   c) Georgia

2. **In 2020, who became a co-host on the television show *Ireland AM*?**
   a) Tommy Bowe
   b) Denis Leamy
   c) Jerry Flannery

3. **What did Australian referee Bob Burnett say to Welsh scrum half Brynmor Williams during Australia's 18–8 victory over Wales in 1978?**
   a) "It's not your ball, Williams, it's ours."
   b) "Don't bother trying. This will be a gold victory."
   c) "I'm not here to let you win."

4. **Naas Botha played 28 Test matches for South Africa as a fly half. What has he had named after him?**
   a) a planet
   b) a rose
   c) a highway

5. **Who was the only player never to be dropped during Clive Woodward's reign as England head coach?**

   a) Jason Leonard

   b) Dan Luger

   c) Richard Hill

6. **Who won a 100th New Zealand cap in 2013?**

   a) Tony Woodcock

   b) Conrad Smith

   c) Kieran Read

7. **Bath were English league champions for the 1991/92 season even though they had a point deducted. Why did they lose a point?**

   a) They played 12 minutes of their home game against Nottingham with 16 players.

   b) They used an ineligible player, Laurie Heatherley, against London Irish.

   c) Their home ground, The Rec, failed a health and safety inspection resulting in the last-minute cancellation of their televised match with Orrell.

8. **Michael Cheika's Australia faced Eddie Jones' England seven times from 2016 to 2019. Which country won all seven encounters?**

9. **Who scored 44 points in Scotland's 89–0 victory over the Ivory Coast at the 1995 Rugby World Cup?**

10. **Eamonn Andrews presented the famous *This Is Your Life* red book to which player following Wales' 12–3 victory over England in 1972?**

Round 31

1. **Who made his Leicester Tigers debut in a game against Bath in 2020?**
   a) Indiana Jones
   b) Harry Potter
   c) Luke Skywalker

2. **In 2014, who became the first Welshman to sign a dual contract with the Welsh Rugby Union?**
   a) Tyler Morgan
   b) Dan Lydiate
   c) Sam Warburton

3. **Prior to 1924, what was the Scottish Rugby Union called?**
   a) Scottish Football Union
   b) Association of Scottish Rugby and Cricket Clubs
   c) Scottish Rugby Committee

4. **Kevin Sinfield was made England's defence coach in 2022. With which rugby league side did he win seven Super League titles?**
   a) Castleford Tigers
   b) Wigan Warriors
   c) Leeds Rhinos

5. **Who was the only other player in Wales' starting XV both when Taulupe Faletau made his International debut, against the Barbarians in 2011, and in his 100th appearance, against France in 2023?**

    a) Ken Owens

    b) Rhys Priestland

    c) George North

6. **For which Super Rugby side did Tana Umaga score 47 tries in 122 appearances from 1996 until 2007?**

    a) Crusaders

    b) Highlanders

    c) Hurricanes

7. **Thierry Lacroix set a France record of eight successful penalty kicks in a match in 1995. Who were the opposition?**

    a) South Africa

    b) Ireland

    c) Scotland

8. **Following Ireland's 18–9 victory over England in 1973, which member of the England team said, "Well, we might not be any good, but at least we turned up."?**

9. **During the 1960s and 1970s, which Wales flanker scored a club record 933 points for London Welsh?**

10. **Which city hosted the 2013 Rugby World Cup Sevens?**

Round 32

1. **John Kirwan, Kevin Skinner and Has Catley all played International rugby for which country?**
    a) New Zealand
    b) France
    c) Argentina

2. **How many caps did Chester Williams earn in a seven-year career for South Africa?**
    a) 27
    b) 34
    c) 41

3. **Fijian centre Seru Rabeni played for which English club side from 2004 until 2009?**
    a) Leeds Carnegie
    b) Leicester Tigers
    c) Gloucester

4. **Dick Thornett won International caps for Australia in both rugby union and league. He also represented his country at the 1960 Rome Olympics. What sport did he compete in?**
    a) sailing
    b) fencing
    c) water polo

5. **In 2007, who was banned for life, later reduced to five years, for assaulting an Ulster fan during a European Cup match between Toulouse and the men from the north of Ireland?**

   a) Yannick Bru
   b) Clément Poitrenaud
   c) Trevor Brennan

6. **Who in 2021 appeared in the BBC's 19th series of *Strictly Come Dancing*?**

   a) Scott Quinnell
   b) Tommy Seymour
   c) Ugo Monye

7. **Which of the following scored the most International tries?**

   a) Émile Ntamack
   b) Christophe Dominici
   c) Christian Darrouy

8. **Which country during the 2019 Rugby World Cup achieved a first ever victory over Ireland?**

9. **England's 1990 win over Argentina is remembered for Federico Méndez's thunderous right-hook, which knocked out an England forward. Who was his victim?**

10. **The British and Irish Lions won their 1997 tour of South Africa by two Tests to one. Which Irish forward was voted players' player of the tour?**

Round 33

1. **Which of the following Joneses was the first to make his International debut?**
   - a) Luke for Australia
   - b) Chris for England
   - c) Ryan for Wales

2. **Which country performs the Sipi Tau war dance before games?**
   - a) Tonga
   - b) Japan
   - c) Cook Islands

3. **Who scored a try on his International debut, as Scotland beat England 20–17 in the 2022 Six Nations Championship?**
   - a) Sam Skinner
   - b) Sione Tuipulotu
   - c) Ben White

4. **Who did former Springbok coach Andre Markgraaff call the "Eric Cantona of South Africa rugby" due to his controversial actions?**
   - a) Pieter Muller
   - b) Adriaan Richter
   - c) James Small

5. **How many International conversions were kicked in total by Luigi Troiani (1985–1995), Didier Camberabero (1982–1993) and Arwel Thomas (1996–2000)?**

    a) 119
    b) 135
    c) 158

6. **The Super Rugby Championship was won by a South African side for the first time in 2007. Who were the champions?**

    a) Bulls
    b) Stormers
    c) Sharks

7. **In 1934, who became the first Australia captain to lift the Bledisloe Cup?**

    a) Bill White
    b) Alec Ross
    c) Ron Walden

8. **One-club man Mike Burton made 360 appearances for which side?**

9. **The 1981 film *Chariots of Fire* depicts the story of which Scottish International's gold medal win at the 1924 Olympic Games?**

10. **Which country inflicted a record home loss on England with a 53–10 victory in the 2023 Six Nations tournament?**

Round 34

1. **Italian Internationals Sergio Parisse, Mauro Bergamasco and Diego Domínguez have all played for which side?**
   a) Stade Français
   b) Melbourne Rebels
   c) Wasps

2. **Who scored a South Africa record of 35 points in a single match against Namibia in 2007?**
   a) Morné Steyn
   b) Percy Montgomery
   c) Tonderai Chavhanga

3. **Jonah Lomu scored 37 tries in a 63-cap New Zealand career. Which country did he score the most against?**
   a) Australia
   b) Italy
   c) England

4. **Barry Holmes won six International caps – four for one country, two for another – got married and died, all in 1949. Which countries did he represent?**
   a) New Zealand and Scotland
   b) England and Argentina
   c) Wales and Australia

5. **Which Scotland International was elected to the South Africa parliament in 1974 as a member of the Progressive Party?**

   a) Stewart Wilson
   b) David Chisholm
   c) Gordon Waddell

6. **The Hopetoun Cup is contested by Australia and which other country?**

   a) Scotland
   b) Wales
   c) France

7. **Prop Phil Orr made 58 International appearances for Ireland. Which club did he represent for over two decades?**

   a) Bective Rangers
   b) Old Wesley
   c) Lansdowne

8. **Which South Africa scrum half played in the 1995, 1999 and 2003 Rugby World Cups?**

9. **Who was the England forward that received a red card after just 82 seconds of play, in a match against Ireland during the 2022 Six Nations Championship?**

10. **Why was Andy Powell thrown out of Wales' 2010 Six Nations squad?**

Round 35

1. **Brothers Eddie and Ian Dunn, Robbie and Bruce Deans, and Rico and Hosea Gear have all gained International recognition. Which country have they represented?**

    a) Australia

    b) Tonga

    c) New Zealand

2. **Danie Craven, Kitch Christie and Peter de Villiers have all held the position of head coach for which country?**

    a) Italy

    b) South Africa

    c) Wales

3. **Of the following, which player scored the most points for England?**

    a) Jonathan Webb

    b) Toby Flood

    c) Alan Old

4. **Who retired in 2022 as Leinster's appearance record-holder, having played 280 times for the province?**

    a) Devin Toner

    b) Michael Bent

    c) Fergus McFadden

5. **During the British and Irish Lions tour of New Zealand in 1971, who scored a record six tries in a match for the tourists at Greymouth?**
    a) Mike Gibson
    b) David Duckham
    c) Gerald Davies

6. **Which founding club of the Rugby Football Union also played association football and won the FA Cup in 1880?**
    a) Queen's House
    b) Ravenscourt Park
    c) Clapham Rovers

7. **Singapore lost by a record score of 164–13 in October 1994. Who were the opposition?**
    a) New Zealand
    b) Hong Kong
    c) Japan

8. **Who scored 25 points for Australia in their 35–12 victory over France in the 1999 Rugby World Cup final?**

9. **Which club was the first to provide 100 players to the England national team?**

10. **Which Welsh International appeared as a contestant in the BBC's 2010 series of *Strictly Come Dancing*?**

Round 36

1. **Who captained Ireland a record 83 times from 2002 until 2012?**

    a) Rory Best
    b) Brian O'Driscoll
    c) Simon Easterby

2. **In 2022, which French side won a first ever Top 14 title?**

    a) Montpellier
    b) Carcassonne
    c) Agen

3. **Which of the following scored the most points during their International career?**

    a) Thomas Castaignède
    b) Gérald Merceron
    c) Jean-Baptiste Élissalde

4. **Which of the following won the most Scotland caps?**

    a) Scott Hastings
    b) Jim Renwick
    c) Tom Smith

5. **What do Gareth Edwards, Rory Underwood and Cyril Lowe have in common?**

    a) made 45 consecutive appearances for their country
    b) captained their country on their International debut
    c) scored 18 tries in the Five Nations Championship

6. Tina Turner's 1985 hit 'We don't need another hero' contained backing vocals by a choir from King's House School. Which future England International was a member of the choir?

    a) Joe Worsley
    b) Martin Johnson
    c) Lawrence Dallaglio

7. Which country's players threatened to go on strike prior to their clash with England in the 2023 Six Nations tournament, due to contractual and funding issues?

    a) Ireland
    b) Wales
    c) Scotland

8. Reuben Thorne, Greg Somerville and Wyatt Crockett have each played over 100 matches for the same side. Which team was it?

9. Who became the second player to earn 100 Wales caps, in a 28–31 loss to the Barbarians in 2011?

10. Who made a record 28 consecutive Test appearances for England from 1953 to 1959, helping his country to a first Grand Slam for 29 years in 1957?

Round 37

1. **Which colour shirt do you associate with South Africa?**

   a) red and silver

   b) green and gold

   c) blue and bronze

2. **Who scored a hat-trick of tries against Italy in both the 2019 and 2023 Six Nations Championships?**

   a) Liam Williams

   b) Jonny May

   c) Blair Kinghorn

3. **Which country set a world record for the most-capped pack when their side against Wales in 2014 contained forwards with a total of 587 appearances to their names?**

   a) Ireland

   b) Italy

   c) France

4. **Which New Zealand fly half kicked all 18 points as Toulouse defeated Toulon by 6 points to win the 2012 French Top 14 championship?**

   a) Aaron Cruden

   b) Dan Carter

   c) Luke McAlister

5. In which year did England first earn a Five Nations wooden spoon for losing all tournament games in a season?

    a) 1967

    b) 1970

    c) 1972

6. Who did England defeat 21–9 in the final of the 2014 Women's Rugby World Cup?

    a) Australia

    b) Canada

    c) France

7. In 1939, which country became the first to complete an unbeaten tour of New Zealand, winning seven games and drawing one?

    a) South Africa

    b) Fiji

    c) Australia

8. Following a career that included 62 appearances for France, which 'caveman' announced his retirement in 2014?

9. Who played 25 Tests for Australia from 1980 to 1984, ten of which as captain, making him the first indigenous Australian to lead a national sporting team?

10. Who was the Newport lock that kicked a penalty goal in his only International, to give Wales a 3–3 draw against Ireland in 1951?

Round 38

1. **Marco Bollesan made 47 International appearances from 1963 until 1975, including 37 as captain. Which country did he represent?**

    a) Scotland

    b) Italy

    c) Australia

2. **Adrian Garvey made 28 appearances for South Africa from 1996 to 1999. Which other country did he earn ten caps for?**

    a) Zimbabwe

    b) Namibia

    c) Argentina

3. **Danie Rossouw, George Smith and Todd Clever have all played for which of the following sides?**

    a) Highlanders

    b) Suntory Sungoliath

    c) Saracens

4. **How many years after Jason Leonard became the first prop to earn 100 England caps did Dan Cole become the second?**

    a) 10 years

    b) 15 years

    c) 20 years

5. **Who was the first Munster man to captain Ireland?**
   a) Tom Clifford
   b) John O'Meara
   c) Jim McCarthy

6. **Who made his professional boxing debut with a cruiserweight win over Barry Dunnett in 2013?**
   a) Quade Cooper
   b) Israel Folau
   c) Matt To'omua

7. **England beat New Zealand 15–9 in 1983. Who bulldozed over the line to score his only International try in 25 England matches?**
   a) Maurice Colclough
   b) Steve Bainbridge
   c) Paul Simpson

8. **At which stadium did Wales capture the 1971 Grand Slam with a 5–9 away victory over France?**

9. **Who broke Llanelli hearts with a last-gasp 58-metre penalty to give Leicester Tigers a 13–12 victory against the west Wales side in their semi-final of the 2002 European Cup?**

10. **In 2022, who became the first Englishman to referee 100 Test matches?**

Round 39

1. **New Zealand won the inaugural Rugby World Cup in 1987. Who captained the side to a 29–9 victory over France in the final?**

   a) David Kirk

   b) Gary Whetton

   c) Wayne Shelford

2. **How many International drop goals were achieved in total by Hugo Porta (1971–1990), Barry John (1966–1972) and Ian McGeechan (1972–1979)?**

   a) 34

   b) 44

   c) 54

3. **Which club in 2020 were relegated from the English Premiership due to persistent salary-cap breaches?**

   a) Saracens

   b) Cornish Pirates

   c) Richmond

4. **Of the following wingers, who scored the most International tries?**

   a) Paul Sackey

   b) Trevor Ringland

   c) Craig Joiner

5. **Scotland beat England in the first ever rugby International on 27 March 1871. The game was played at the Academy Ground, Raeburn Place, Edinburgh. How many players were in each side?**

   a) 13
   b) 17
   c) 20

6. **Which member of Argentina's 2007 Rugby World Cup squad was killed in a drive-by shooting in Paris in 2022?**

   a) Ignacio Corleto
   b) Felipe Contepomi
   c) Federico Martín Aramburú

7. **Who captained the New Zealand women's team to a 25–17 win over England in the 2006 Women's Rugby World Cup final?**

   a) Emma Jensen
   b) Farah Palmer
   c) Amiria Marsh

8. **Who scored 64 tries in 101 Tests for Australia from 1982 to 1996?**

9. **Who scored 1,049 points in an 87-cap career for Wales that began with his debut against England in 1991?**

10. **The book *Me and My Mouth* was released in 2006. Which Englishman's autobiography was this?**

Round 40

1. **Who in 2018 named former Scotland captain Jonny Petrie as their Chief Executive Officer?**

    a) Ospreys

    b) Harlequins

    c) Ulster

2. **Welsh Internationals Gerald Davies and Mervyn Davies shared the same real first name. What was it?**

    a) Thomas

    b) Richard

    c) David

3. **Italy won their first ever Six Nations match 34–20 in 2000. Who were the opposition?**

    a) Wales

    b) Scotland

    c) France

4. **Michael Jones made 55 New Zealand Test appearances. Which country did he represent on a single occasion in 1986, prior to his All Black career?**

    a) Tonga

    b) Cook Islands

    c) Samoa

5. **Serge Blanco played his entire career for which club side?**

   a) Brive

   b) Biarritz

   c) Castres

6. **Jack Hartley won a single cap for South Africa in 1891 as a winger. What national record did he set?**

   a) youngest International, at 18 years and 18 days

   b) first player to score four tries in a Test match

   c) first cricket and rugby union dual International

7. **Which England International was hit by a double-decker bus while on a fancy-dress end-of-season pub crawl with Sale Sharks in 2013?**

   a) Danny Cipriani

   b) Henry Thomas

   c) Ben Foden

8. **Who became the tallest man to play International rugby when a Scotland forward made his debut in 2000, standing at seven feet tall?**

9. **Gareth Edwards, Ieuan Evans and Scott Gibbs each went on three British and Irish Lions tours. Which one made the most Test appearances?**

10. **Which country won a first ever Six Nations match in Cardiff during the 2022 tournament?**

Round 41

1. **Bill Dickinson became the first Scotland national coach in 1971. What was his job title?**
   - a) adviser to the captain
   - b) counsel of the president
   - c) consultant to the Scottish Rugby Union

2. **Which Irish second row earned 51 caps for his country from 1974 to 1984?**
   - a) Harold Steele
   - b) Donal Spring
   - c) Moss Keane

3. **All Black International brothers Graeme and Stephen Bachop played against each other twice in 1999. Who did they represent in those games?**
   - a) Japan and Samoa
   - b) Tonga and Fiji
   - c) Italy and Georgia

4. **Wales defeated England 28–6 in Cardiff on 21 January 1922. What was noteworthy about the match?**
   - a) first match broadcast by BBC radio
   - b) last game where a conversion was worth three points
   - c) both teams wore numbers on their jerseys in an International for the first time

5. **Which club won the 1976 and 1977 John Player Cup?**
   a) Moseley
   b) Rosslyn Park
   c) Gosforth

6. **Sias Swart, Lofty Fourie and Jan Ellis are the only three players to have represented South Africa while playing for which side?**
   a) Border State
   b) South West Africa
   c) North East Territory

7. **Prior to Wales' game against Scotland in the 1971 Five Nations tournament, why did Clive Rowlands have to speed back to the team hotel on a police motorbike?**
   a) Gareth Edwards had forgotten his gum shield.
   b) The team shirts had been left in the hotel lobby.
   c) Denzil Williams had lost his boots.

8. **Which Australia outside half, with Nick Farr-Jones during the 1980s and 1990s, set a 47-Test world record for a half back combination?**

9. **Why was Wales attack coach Rob Howley given an 18-month suspension from rugby union in 2019?**

10. **In 1925 Cyril Brownlie of New Zealand became the first person to be sent off against England. It took 55 years for the next player to be sent off against the English. Who was he?**

Round 42

1. **What colour shirt did England wear in a match against Wales in February 2010 to celebrate 100 years of International rugby at Twickenham?**

   a) cream

   b) green

   c) pink

2. **Who captained Scotland to 1999 Five Nations Championship victory?**

   a) Stuart Grimes

   b) Alan Tait

   c) Gary Armstrong

3. **Who scored a brace of tries on his Italy debut, in a 22–33 loss to Scotland in 2022?**

   a) Leonardo Marin

   b) Alessandro Fusco

   c) Ange Capuozzo

4. **In 2002, which side became the first to win every match in a Super Rugby season?**

   a) Waratahs

   b) Crusaders

   c) Brumbies

5. **Va'aiga Tuigamala earned 41 International caps, scoring 8 tries. 19 of these appearances were for New Zealand – which other country did he play for?**

   a) Samoa

   b) Tonga

   c) Australia

6. **Which centre earned a 50th Ireland cap in a match against Scotland in 2023?**

   a) Bundee Aki

   b) Robbie Henshaw

   c) Garry Ringrose

7. **Who scored Wales' only try as they defeated England by a margin of 3 points at the 2015 Rugby World Cup?**

   a) Wyn Jones

   b) Gareth Davies

   c) Scott Williams

8. **Which Australia flanker received a formal written warning from the Australian Rugby Union in 2014 for being arrested at a coalmine protest in New South Wales?**

9. **Who was the only London Welsh player on the British and Irish Lions tour of New Zealand in 1977?**

10. **Who was the only South Africa player to appear in both their 1995 and 2007 Rugby World Cup-winning sides?**

Round 43

1. **How many rugby Internationals lost their lives in the First World War?**
    - a) 56
    - b) 89
    - c) 111

2. **England defeated Fiji 58–23 in 1989. Who during the game became the second Englishman to score five tries in a match?**
    - a) Mark Bailey
    - b) Jeremy Guscott
    - c) Rory Underwood

3. **Who scored four tries for Scotland against France in January 1925, then another four tries against Wales the following month?**
    - a) Ian Smith
    - b) Johnnie Wallace
    - c) Dan Drysdale

4. **England and New Zealand played out a 25–25 draw at Twickenham in 2022. Who made his 100th appearance for the away side in the encounter?**
    - a) Aaron Smith
    - b) Brodie Retallick
    - c) Rieko Ioane

5. **Who did Wales defeat 72–18 in their opening match of the 2007 Rugby World Cup?**

    a) Japan

    b) Namibia

    c) Romania

6. **Father and son Guy and Didier Camberabero achieved which identical International record?**

    a) 36 France appearances

    b) 11 drop goals

    c) 6 tries

7. **Who played the role of 'Frank the bookie' in the 2001 film *Very Annie Mary*?**

    a) Graham Price

    b) Ray Gravell

    c) Mark Ring

8. **Which future global superstar became the youngest Test All Black in 1994, at the age of 19 years and 45 days?**

9. **Which member of Scotland's 1990 Grand Slam-winning side had a New Zealand International father?**

10. **Which BBC commentator, who died in 2022 while doing a charity hike in Peru, made his Wales debut in an 18–9 victory over France in 1980?**

Round 44

1. **Antoine Dupont made his France debut in a match against Italy in 2017. Which club was he playing for at the time?**
   a) Auch
   b) Castres
   c) Bath

2. **Who retired in 2022 as the English Premiership's all-time appearance record-holder?**
   a) Phil Dowson
   b) Richard Wigglesworth
   c) Tom May

3. **Who was the only other player to appear in England's starting XV for both Brian Moore's first cap in 1987 and his final International match in 1995?**
   a) Rory Underwood
   b) Rob Andrew
   c) Dean Richards

4. **Who scored a brace of tries in South Africa's 37–13 Rugby World Cup semi-final win over Argentina in 2007?**
   a) J P Pietersen
   b) Fourie du Preez
   c) Bryan Habana

5. **Harlequins forward Wavell Wakefield won three Grand Slams with England in the 1920s. What did he become after retiring from rugby?**

    a) a Baptist missionary in Nigeria
    b) a Conservative Member of Parliament in the UK
    c) the Prime Minister of Jamaica

6. **Irish fly half Jack Kyle played provincial rugby for which side?**

    a) Ulster
    b) Munster
    c) Leinster

7. **How many International tries were scored in total by David Venditti (1996–2000), Martin Leslie (1998–2003) and Simon Geoghegan (1991–1996)?**

    a) 27
    b) 33
    c) 39

8. **Who was the South Africa International scrum half that made 141 appearances for Ulster from 2010 to 2017?**

9. **Which two players appeared in Australia's starting line-up for both the 1991 and 1999 Rugby World Cup finals?**

10. **Which future successful businessman made the last of 40 Ireland appearances in their 32–4 loss to Wales in 1975?**

Round 45

1. **Which country became the first to achieve a third consecutive Five Nations Triple Crown with a 20–16 victory over Ireland in 1978?**

    a) Scotland

    b) Wales

    c) England

2. **Who beat New Zealand 17–12 to win Commonwealth Games Sevens gold in 2014?**

    a) Fiji

    b) Wales

    c) South Africa

3. **Which country defeated New Zealand 19–7 at the semi-final stage of the 2019 Rugby World Cup?**

    a) England

    b) Wales

    c) Scotland

4. **What controversial act did Tonga's Epi Taione carry out before the 2007 Rugby World Cup?**

    a) requested King George V stand down due to the disparity in wealth between the royal family and the average person in Tonga

    b) changed his name by deed poll to Paddy Power as part of a sponsorship deal with the bookmaker

    c) changed allegiance to New Zealand, playing in three matches for the All Blacks

5. **Which referee was attacked on the pitch by a South Africa fan during a 2002 International between the Springboks and All Blacks?**

   a) Joël Jutge
   b) Chris White
   c) David McHugh

6. **Who became the first British player to lift the European Cup, captaining Bath to glory in 1998?**

   a) Phil de Glanville
   b) Richard Webster
   c) Andy Nicol

7. **Who scored 25 points as Argentina beat England by a one-point margin at Twickenham in 2022?**

   a) Emiliano Boffelli
   b) Santiago Carreras
   c) Juan Cruz Mallía

8. **Steve Phillips resigned as Chief Executive Officer of which country's union in 2023 following a BBC programme raising allegations of misogyny, sexism, racism and homophobia within the governing body?**

9. **Which Dutch-born winger made his debut for Scotland through the three-year residency rule in 2012?**

10. **Which All Black outside half scored 291 points in 35 Test matches following his debut against Argentina in 1997?**

Round 46

1. **Which of the following had the highest win percentage in an Ireland shirt?**

    a) Brian O'Driscoll

    b) Peter Stringer

    c) Mike Gibson

2. **Which Welshman received a red card for a tip tackle 18 minutes into Wales' 2011 Rugby World Cup semi-final match against France?**

    a) Sam Warburton

    b) Mike Phillips

    c) Alun Wyn Jones

3. **Scotland used their first ever substitute in a match against France in 1969. Who was the player who took to the field that day?**

    a) Ian McCrane

    b) Colin Blaikie

    c) Wilson Lauder

4. **The Antim Cup is contested between which two nations?**

    a) USA and Canada

    b) Italy and Spain

    c) Georgia and Romania

5. **Who lost to a Rugby World Cup record score of 142–0 against Australia in 2003?**

   a) Portugal
   b) Namibia
   c) Spain

6. **Which club produced future England Internationals Danny Grewcock, Neil Back and Tom Wood?**

   a) Walsall
   b) Berkswell and Balsall
   c) Barkers' Butts

7. **Sammy Walker, Robin Thompson and Colin Patterson were all Irish Internationals. Which club did they play for?**

   a) Portadown
   b) Instonians
   c) Ballyclare

8. **South Africa defeated England 15–6 in the 2007 Rugby World Cup final. Who was the winning captain?**

9. **Why did Graham Mourie receive a ten-year ban from playing or coaching rugby?**

10. **Which country won the inaugural Rugby World Cup Sevens in 1993?**

Round 47

1. **Back-row forwards Josh Sole, Alessandro Zanni and Aaron Persico have all played International rugby. Which country have they represented?**
   a) Australia
   b) Namibia
   c) Italy

2. **Whose dramatic late try gave Wales a 20–19 victory over France at the quarter-final stage of the 2019 Rugby World Cup?**
   a) Ross Moriarty
   b) Jake Ball
   c) Leigh Halfpenny

3. **Who captained New Zealand to a disappointing 1999 Rugby World Cup semi-final loss to France at Twickenham?**
   a) Anton Oliver
   b) Taine Randell
   c) Byron Kelleher

4. **Tony Stanger scored a decisive try in Scotland's 13–7 victory over England in 1990, providing his side with a third Grand Slam. Who made an under-pressure chip-kick to create the try?**
   a) Gary Armstrong
   b) Craig Chalmers
   c) Gavin Hastings

5. **Who scored 13 tries in 37 Australia appearances after a high-profile switch from rugby league in 2001?**

    a) Wendell Sailor

    b) Andrew Walker

    c) Lote Tuqiri

6. **Ernest Hammett, William Hancock and Colin Smart all won England caps while playing for which Welsh club side?**

    a) Swansea

    b) Newport

    c) Pontypool

7. **Queensland Country Bank Stadium hosted the 100th clash between which two countries in 2021?**

    a) New Zealand and South Africa

    b) Ireland and Fiji

    c) England and Scotland

8. **Which side became the first to win back-to-back Hong Kong Sevens Cup finals in 1977 and 1978?**

9. **Which Irish province in 2016 clinched their first Pro12 title with a 20–10 victory over Leinster in the final?**

10. **France beat New Zealand 16–3 in 1986. What happened to Wayne Shelford in the match?**

Round 48

1. **Patrick Estève, Fabien Galthié and Mathieu Bastareaud have all played International rugby. Which country have they represented?**
   - a) Italy
   - b) France
   - c) Spain

2. **Which club won their first Welsh Rugby Union Challenge Cup in 2018 with a 41–7 victory over Newport?**
   - a) Merthyr
   - b) Cross Keys
   - c) Pontypool

3. **Who is England International forwards Tom and Ben Curry's uncle?**
   - a) Mike Teague
   - b) Rob Andrew
   - c) John Olver

4. **Which English club side did Australian International Michael Lynagh join in 1996?**
   - a) Bath
   - b) Saracens
   - c) Harlequins

5. **Who was the twice-capped England wing named in Scotland's 2023 Six Nations squad?**

   a) Tom Collins

   b) Josh Bassett

   c) Ruaridh McConnochie

6. **Schalk Burger made his South Africa debut in 2003. Which side did he play for at the time?**

   a) Boland Cavaliers

   b) Western Province

   c) Golden Lions

7. **On 12 July 2011, which former Wales flanker set a world record for becoming the first person to climb the highest mountain on each of the world's seven continents and stand on the North Pole, South Pole and summit of Mount Everest within a seven-month period?**

   a) Richard Parks

   b) Colin Charvis

   c) Richie Collins

8. **Which club won the Scottish National League Division One title for five consecutive years during the 1970s?**

9. **Which Canadian winger won the 2001 European Cup final with the Leicester Tigers?**

10. **Which Rugby World Cup-winning All Black received a four-week ban for the start of the 2012 Super Rugby season after a naked, drunken rampage in the Cook Islands?**

Round 49

1. **How many International points were scored in total by Jonathan Davies (1985–1997), Brendan Mullin (1984–1995) and John Eales (1991–2001)?**

    a) 326

    b) 418

    c) 523

2. **What was distinctive about Doug Howlett's appearance in New Zealand's 40–8 win over Ireland in 2002?**

    a) He was the first All Black to score a hat-trick of tries in three consecutive games.

    b) He was the only non-Crusaders player in the side.

    c) He was the first All Black to start a match in four different positions within the same season.

3. **England centre Manu Tuilagi was fined close to £8,000 during the 2011 Rugby World Cup. Which of the following indiscretions did he <u>not</u> commit?**

    a) He wore a sponsored mouth guard.

    b) He jumped off a ferry in Auckland.

    c) He set off the hotel fire alarm.

4. **Which of the following Irish outside halves made the most British and Irish Lions Test appearances?**

    a) Ollie Campbell

    b) Ronan O'Gara

    c) Tony Ward

5. **Who made 33 consecutive appearances in a Wales jersey over a 12-year period, starting with a loss to Scotland in 1890?**

   a) Arthur Gould
   b) Billy Bancroft
   c) Selwyn Biggs

6. **Who was the only 20th-century British and Irish Lions captain to win a series after losing the opening Test?**

   a) Willie John McBride
   b) Phil Bennett
   c) Finlay Calder

7. **Which of the following Scotland Internationals' father led a team which protected South African President Nelson Mandela?**

   a) Rob Wainwright
   b) Simon Danielli
   c) Kyle Steyn

8. **In which year was the first ever Six Nations match between the two highest-ranked teams in the world?**

9. **Sanivalati Laulau set a national record of 20 tries in 32 matches when he retired in 1985. Which country did he play for?**

10. **Wales lost 6–9 to England in Cardiff in 1947. What was unique about England wing Dickie Guest and Wales full back Howard Davies and scrum half Haydn Tanner?**

Round 50

1. **Which of the following is a type of freshwater fish?**
    a) Cliff Morgan
    b) Jack Dempsey
    c) Dean Richards

2. **Who set a record that stood for almost two decades for the most consecutive Tests played in an England jersey, with 36 appearances from 1968 to 1975?**
    a) Keith Fairbrother
    b) David Duckham
    c) John Pullin

3. **Cardiff played Australia six times in the 20th century. How many times did the Welsh side win?**
    a) twice
    b) four times
    c) all six games

4. **Why were three pool matches cancelled at the 2019 Rugby World Cup?**
    a) Covid-19 outbreak in Yokohama
    b) health and safety concerns caused by Typhoon Hagibis
    c) Namibia being removed from the competition due to political interference

5. **Which of the following 'near-death' experiences did Scotland International Mike Campbell-Lamerton not have?**

    a) shark attack off the Florida coast

    b) struck in the chest by a javelin

    c) standing on a mine in the Far East while on army duty

6. **Which two players scored a brace of tries each in Scotland's 29–23 victory over England at Twickenham in the 2023 Six Nations Championship?**

    a) Max Malins and Duhan van der Merwe

    b) Maro Itoje and Finn Russell

    c) Freddie Steward and Luke Crosbie

7. **England defeated Australia 9–6 at Twickenham in 1958. Who scored a 60-yard try late in the game to give the home side victory?**

    a) Jim Hetherington

    b) Peter Jackson

    c) Jeff Butterfield

8. **Which Argentina back-row forward won the 2013 and 2014 European Cup with Toulon?**

9. **Who was the New Zealand outside half that set a 45-point national record for a single match on his debut against Japan in 1995?**

10. **Who was the British and Irish Lions player upended by Tana Umaga and Keven Mealamu in the first Test against New Zealand in 2005, resulting in the target dislocating his shoulder and missing the remainder of the series?**

Answers

Round 1

1. a
2. c
3. b
4. a
5. c
6. c
7. a
8. Michel Hooper
9. Phil Bennett
10. Brad Thorn (2011 Rugby World Cup with New Zealand, 2008 Super Rugby with Crusaders, 2012 European Cup with Leinster)

Round 2

1. a
2. c
3. c (against Japan)
4. c
5. b
6. a
7. a
8. Johnny Sexton
9. Geoff Cooke
10. Scotland

Round 3

1. c
2. b

3. a
4. a
5. c
6. b
7. a
8. Ian Smith (Scotland)
9. Llanelli
10. Marc Cécillon

Round 4

1. c
2. a
3. b
4. c
5. a
6. b
7. a
8. Gary and Alan Whetton
9. South Africa
10. Wasps and Worcester Warriors

Round 5

1. a
2. a (Alain Penaud won 32 caps, Peter Clohessy won 54 caps and Paul Thorburn won 37)
3. c
4. c
5. b
6. a
7. b (a 28–27 victory)
8. Roy Laidlaw
9. André Joubert
10. Northampton

Round 6

1. b
2. a
3. c
4. a
5. c
6. c
7. b
8. Hugo Porta
9. Keith Wood
10. Siya Kolisi

Round 7

1. c
2. a
3. b
4. c
5. a (Michael Kiernan scored 308 points for Ireland, Bob Hiller scored 138 points for England and Gavin Henson scored 130 points for Wales)
6. b
7. b
8. Regan King
9. Neil Back
10. Graham Henry

Round 8

1. b
2. c
3. a
4. b
5. b
6. c

7. c
8. Finn Russell
9. Richie McCaw
10. Bryan Habana

Round 9

1. a
2. b
3. c
4. b
5. a
6. c
7. a
8. Rassie Erasmus
9. Grant Fox
10. Courtney Lawes and Dan Biggar

Round 10

1. b
2. c
3. a
4. b
5. a
6. c
7. a (Phil Bennett won eight caps, Paul O'Connell won seven caps and John Jeffrey won one cap)
8. centre
9. Steve Hansen
10. Waisale Serevi

Round 11

1. a
2. a

3. b
4. c
5. c
6. b
7. a
8. Earn a 100th cap for Australia
9. Hawick
10. England

Round 12

1. c
2. a
3. b
4. b
5. a
6. a
7. c
8. Israel Folau
9. Mike Catt
10. Clive Burgess

Round 13

1. a
2. b
3. c
4. b
5. a
6. c
7. b
8. Alun Wyn Jones
9. Tom Kiernan
10. Josh Kronfeld

Round 14

1. b
2. c
3. b
4. c
5. a
6. a
7. b
8. Ireland and Italy
9. Gareth Davies and David Richards
10. boxing

Round 15

1. c
2. a
3. c
4. a
5. b
6. c
7. a (Josh Adams scored seven tries, Makazole Mapimpi scored six tries and Kotaro Matsushima scored five tries)
8. Portugal
9. Andy Leslie
10. Alex Lozowski (his father was Rob Lozowski)

Round 16

1. a
2. c
3. b
4. a
5. b

6. c
7. c
8. Gavin Hastings
9. Pontypool
10. Dan Carter

Round 17

1. b
2. a
3. c
4. c
5. a
6. a
7. a (this was a record for a lock)
8. Stuart Hogg
9. John Kirwan
10. Mauro and Mirco Bergamasco

Round 18

1. c
2. b
3. a
4. c
5. a
6. b
7. c
8. Tom Kiernan
9. Arthur Smith
10. Ruan Pienaar

Round 19

1. c
2. b

3. a
4. c
5. b (the record stood for five years)
6. a
7. a
8. J P R Williams
9. Scotland
10. Nelson Mandela

Round 20

1. a
2. b
3. c
4. b
5. c
6. b
7. c
8. Bryan Williams
9. Wayne Pivac
10. Gareth Rees

Round 21

1. a
2. b
3. a
4. a
5. b
6. c
7. a
8. Josh van der Flier
9. Terry Price
10. Bill McLaren

Round 22

1. b
2. a
3. a
4. c
5. b
6. b
7. c
8. Bill Beaumont (the Bill Beaumont Cup)
9. They were each their country's 1000th-capped International player
10. Tana Umaga (New Zealand) and Mike Umaga (Samoa)

Round 23

1. b
2. c
3. a
4. c
5. b
6. a
7. c
8. South Africa
9. Émile Ntamack
10. Dusty Hare

Round 24

1. b
2. b
3. c
4. b (John Taylor won 4 caps, Jeff Squire won 6 caps and Derek Quinnell won 5 caps)

5. a
6. c
7. a
8. Limerick
9. Victor Matfield
10. cricket

Round 25

1. b
2. c
3. b (Piet Uys won 12 caps, Dawie de Villiers won 25 caps and Dick Lockyear won 6 caps)
4. a
5. c
6. a
7. b
8. Uruguay
9. Agustín Pichot
10. Andy Dalton (Andy Dalton won 35 caps, Ray Dalton won 2 caps)

Round 26

1. b
2. c
3. a
4. a (Malcolm O'Kelly won 92 caps, Mark Taylor won 52 caps and Olivier Roumat won 61 caps)
5. c
6. b
7. c
8. Sale Sharks
9. Cliff Morgan
10. La Rochelle

Round 27

1. a
2. a
3. c
4. b
5. a
6. b
7. c
8. Sonny Bill Williams
9. Sam Burgess
10. Drew Mitchell

Round 28

1. b
2. c
3. a
4. c
5. a (the Tier One side being Italy)
6. b
7. c
8. Clermont Auvergne
9. Tom Curry
10. New Zealand

Round 29

1. b
2. c
3. a
4. b
5. c (Seán O'Brien scored 1 try, Rory Underwood scored 1 try, Gerald Davies scored 3 tries)
6. c

7. a
8. six (five missed tackles plus a tackle two metres out, but his momentum carried him across the line)
9. Connacht
10. Rex Richards

Round 30

1. b
2. a
3. a
4. b (Rosa Naas Botha)
5. c
6. a
7. b
8. England
9. Gavin Hastings
10. Barry John

Round 31

1. b
2. c
3. a
4. c
5. c
6. c
7. b
8. John Pullin
9. John Taylor
10. Moscow

Round 32

1. a

2. a
3. b
4. c
5. c
6. c
7. a (Émile Ntamack scored 26 tries, Christophe Dominici scored 25 tries and Christian Darrouy scored 23 tries)
8. Japan (a 19–12 victory)
9. Paul Ackford
10. Jeremy Davidson

Round 33

1. b (Luke Jones made his International debut in June 2014, Chris Jones in February 2004 and Ryan Jones in November 2004)
2. a
3. c
4. c
5. b (Luigi Troiani scored 57 conversions, Didier Camberabero scored 48 conversions and Arwel Thomas scored 30 conversions)
6. a
7. b
8. Gloucester
9. Eric Liddell
10. France

Round 34

1. a
2. b
3. c (8 tries)
4. b
5. c
6. a

7. b
8. Joost van der Westhuizen
9. Charlie Ewels
10. He drove a golf buggy on the M4 motorway while drunk, looking for breakfast.

Round 35

1. c
2. b
3. b (Jonathan Webb scored 296 points, Toby Ford scored 301 points, while Alan Old scored 98 points)
4. a
5. b
6. c
7. b
8. Matt Burke
9. Blackheath
10. Gavin Henson

Round 36

1. b
2. a
3. b (Thomas Castaignède scored 247 points, Gérald Merceron scored 267 points and Jean-Baptiste Élissalde scored 214 points)
4. a (Scott Hastings won 65 caps, Jim Renwick won 52 caps and Tom Smith won 61 caps)
5. c
6. c
7. b
8. Crusaders
9. Stephen Jones
10. Jeff Butterfield

Round 37

1. b
2. c
3. b
4. c
5. c
6. b
7. b
8. Sébastien Chabal
9. Mark Ella
10. Ben Edwards

Round 38

1. b
2. a
3. b
4. c
5. c
6. a
7. a
8. Stade de Colombes
9. Tim Stimpson
10. Wayne Barnes

Round 39

1. a
2. b (Hugo Porta scored 26 drop goals, Barry John scored 10 drop goals [including 2 for the British and Irish Lions] and Ian McGeechan scored 8 drop goals [including 1 for the British and Irish Lions])
3. a
4. a (Paul Sackey scored 11 tries, Trevor Ringland scored 9 tries and Craig Joiner scored 3 tries)

5. c
6. c
7. b
8. David Campese
9. Neil Jenkins
10. Austin Healey

Round 40

1. c
2. a
3. b
4. c
5. b
6. a
7. a
8. Richard Metcalfe
9. Gareth Edwards (Gareth Edwards made 10 appearances, Ieuan Evans made 7 appearances and Scott Gibbs made 5 appearances)
10. Italy

Round 41

1. a
2. c
3. a (Graeme Bachop for Japan, Stephen Bachop for Samoa)
4. c
5. c
6. b
7. a
8. Michael Lynagh
9. For breaching betting regulations
10. Paul Ringer (Wales)

Round 42

1. a
2. c
3. c
4. b
5. a
6. c
7. b
8. David Pocock
9. Alun Lewis
10. Os du Randt

Round 43

1. c
2. c
3. a
4. b
5. a
6. b
7. b
8. Jonah Lomu
9. Sean Lineen (his father was Terry Lineen)
10. Eddie Butler

Round 44

1. b
2. b
3. a
4. c
5. b
6. a
7. a (David Venditti scored 6 tries, Martin Leslie scored 10 tries and Simon Geoghegan scored 11 tries)

8. Graham Henry
9. Tim Horan and John Eales
10. Ray McLoughlin

Round 45

1. b
2. c
3. a
4. b
5. c
6. c
7. a
8. Wales
9. Tim Visser
10. Carlos Spencer

Round 46

1. b (Brian O'Driscoll had a 61% win rate, Peter Stringer had a 69% win rate and Mike Gibson had a 49% win rate)
2. a
3. a
4. c
5. b
6. c
7. b
8. John Smit
9. He accepted royalties from his 1982 autobiography. This was classified as an act of professionalism.
10. England

Round 47

1. c
2. a
3. b
4. c
5. a
6. b
7. a (New Zealand won 19–17)
8. Fiji
9. Connacht
10. He lost four teeth and ripped his scrotum, which he had the physio stitch up so that he could return to the field. He then had a blow to the head that forced him off with concussion.

Round 48

1. b
2. a
3. c
4. b
5. c
6. b
7. a
8. Hawick
9. Winston Stanley
10. Zac Guildford

Round 49

1. a (Jonathan Davies scored 81 points, Brendan Mullin scored 72 points and John Eales scored 173 points)
2. b
3. c

4. a (Ollie Campbell made 7 appearances, Ronan O'Gara made 2 appearances and Tony Ward made a single appearance)
5. b
6. c
7. c
8. 2023 (Ireland were ranked 1st and France were ranked 2nd at the time of their Six Nations clash)
9. Fiji
10. They were the only previously capped players in the teams, due to the hiatus caused by the Second World War.

Round 50

1. b
2. c
3. c
4. b
5. a
6. a
7. b
8. Juan Martín Fernández Lobbe
9. Simon Culhane
10. Brian O'Driscoll

Also by the author:

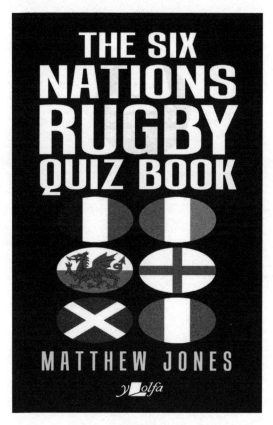

£4.99